Growin' Up

Snapshots/fragments

by

John Sills

1

Contents

Introduction

Fragments, shards, scattered memories...

Growin' up.

I'm not sure if you'd call these poems. They don't rhyme much. But what's a poem? What's not? Does it matter? I started writing with an idea in mind and this is what came out.

These are snapshots of my life up to the age of 25. Fragments of memory, the sort of thing that might appear in your thoughts for no obvious reason. Or in your dreams, mangled up with all sorts of other stuff. Certain things stay with you, even if they aren't that important in themselves. Together they build a picture of who you were, who you are. Memories that shape your responses to things even today. Still explanations for how you feel. Embedded, resonant.

Reassembling these fragments, I felt like I was understanding myself more – even myself today, thirty, forty, fifty years on.

They are sketches in time, blurred by time. But occasionally brought into sharp focus. They may be faulty memories, but they reflect deep feelings. You never forget those feelings, even when you can't quite make sense of them.

These are my experiences. You may have similar ones. But they'll never be the same. We all move in a slightly different dimension of space and time. We recollect the same thing in different ways when we have interacted. But memories can still be shared, celebrated, even when they are different.

So I hope this selection of my memories can be enjoyed and related to, stirring memories of your own.

Together, they tell a story.

John Sills
July 2017

Growin' Up

You never stop growing up,
But you slow down.
And maybe don't realise
You are still learning.
Every day, new facts,
New experiences,
To be treasured.
If you think about it.
Bruce Springsteen
Had a song called "Growin' Up"
On "Greetings from Asbury Park NJ".
Proper Bruce fans never forget
The "NJ".
He has a song for most
Of the important
Things in life.

Christmas morning

I was born
On Christmas morning
1958.
A month early.
How inconvenient.
At 3.30 am.
How very inconvenient.

It was in Central Middlesex hospital,
Which is in Acton
West London.
Near East Acton tube station,
On the Central Line.
It is not in Middlesex,
As far as I am aware.

The midwife was Irish.
She said to my Mum,
"You should call him Jesus".
They called me John,
After my Dad.
Not after the Baptist,
Or the disciple,
As far as I am aware.

Most of my friends
From the same generation,
The late fifties kids,
Are called John (or Jon)
Or Dave,
If they're not John.
There wasn't much choice

In those days.

But we're OK with that.

Cow in the garden

When I was three
I lived in Ventor,
On the Isle of Wight,
With my Mum.
My Dad was in Nigeria,
Fixing radios
On aircraft.
Fighting, I assume,
In the Biafran War.
All I knew then was that we were in
The Isle of Wight,
And he was in Nigeria.
In fact,
I'm not even sure if I knew that.
I just knew
We were here,
And he was there.

One day there was a cow
In our garden.
This is the first thing
I remember vividly
About my life.
It was just munching the grass,
Doing no-one any harm.
How it got there,
I don't know.
There was no hole in our fence
That I could see.
But it was there,
Munching the grass.

My Mum was in
A bit of a state
About it.
I guess I would be,
As an adult, too.

I have no memory
Of how the cow
Was removed.
The next thing I remember
About Ventor
Is being hit on the head
With a plastic hammer
On a grassy slope,
Near the house.
By whom,
I can't remember.
It might have been a girl.

Law abiding citizen

I was five or maybe six,
I had a blue plastic hammer.
You bang things with hammers.
Drive in nails,
Or smash things.
We had a fire alarm thing
Outside our house,
With a little glass plate,
Just asking to be smashed.
With a blue plastic hammer.
One day I did it.
No-one noticed.
I went off to play in the park,
Climb trees,
Not very well.
I heard a noise,
A fire engine,
Getting closer.
Sounded like it was near our house.
I hid in the tree,
Not that far up,
As I wasn't good at climbing.
Didn't have a head for heights.
Regretted smashing that glass thing.
Why else was there a fire siren
Near our house?
I went home after a while,
Mum said the fire engine
Had been round.
Someone had smashed the glass.
No-one had seen it,
No-one knew who it was.

Various boys were suspected.
Not me.
I said nothing except
Er, that's strange,
Or something like that.
I can't remember exactly.
I was worried.
Would they have an investigation?
Would I be questioned?
Would Mum suspect me?
Had I gone red?
I didn't know.
I resolved to say nothing,
And nothing ever happened.
But I never did anything like that
Again.

That day I became
A law abiding citizen.

Miss Williams the Unjust

My first school was in Suffolk.
Ringshall was its name.
We had a teacher
Called Miss Williams.
She kept me in class
While everyone else played football,
Because I helped another boy
With his maths.
She told us to keep quiet,
But I'd finished,
And he couldn't do it.
So I told him how,
And got punished for it.
What was that all about?
My first brush
With injustice,
As dispensed
By those in authority.
I've railed against those in authority
Ever since,
Even when I'm in authority,
If that makes any sense.
Can I blame Miss Williams?
Probably not,
But maybe I can thank her
For contributing to my strong sense
Of injustice.

Thunderbirds

I loved Thunderbirds.
I was obsessed with Thunderbirds.
Virgil Tracey and Thunderbird 2
Were my favourites.
But I had all the models.
Many of the great TV episodes
Involved the Mole.
Only Thunderbird 2
Could transport it,
In one of its pods.
Likewise Thunderbird 4,
The underwater one.
So Thunderbird 2
Made it all happen.
Of course the whole team mattered,
Except maybe,
Thunderbird 3,
Which was a luxury,
As it only went into space,
And there wasn't much call
For that.
There were a set of
Bubblegum cards,
Black and white photos,
All the classic scenes,
120 or so.
I wasn't allowed bubblegum
But somehow got
All the cards.
Chewed the bubblegum,
First bite was lovely,
Sugary.

Spat it out
Before I got home.
Traded for the last few cards.
A lot of bubblegum
When I wasn't allowed.
A blind eye
May have been turned.

Gary

We'd sit in the carob trees,
Gary and me,
Discussing the girls we liked
In our class,
And who we'd dance with
At the Island Club disco.
We were only ten,
Or maybe eleven,
But Cyprus set us free.
It was the most confident
I ever felt about girls,
Ever.
And so they danced with me,
Willingly,
And Gary too,
Probably.
But I can't remember
Anything about that.

Wendy

At the Island Club disco
In Limassol,
For ten and eleven year olds,
I felt like the disco king,
Before there were disco kings.
Cravat, paisley shirt, long trousers.
John Travolta,
Before John Travolta.
I danced with Wendy,
Twenty six times.
Or so I remember.
I was counting,
That's for sure.
She had a broken arm,
In a cast,
And lovely dark hair.
Long and wavy,
It smelled nice,
She was beautiful.
We did slow dances,
I looked after her arm.
Love Grows as My Rosemary goes
Was one of the songs,
But what were the other 25?
I sometimes wonder whether
It is a false memory,
But I don't think so.
Just a treasured memory,
Because I never felt so confident
With a girl again,
Like I did with
Wendy.

Romans, Normans, Saxons and Vikings

Our school in Limassol,
For the expats,
The RAF kids mostly,
Was called Campbell School.
If it was named after someone
It was obviously
Someone called Campbell.
But Who Campbell,
Or Campbell Who,
I've no idea.
Our teacher in the sixth form
Was Mr Birch.
He had a beard and was
Really good
At art.
And lots of other stuff too.
We all liked him.
He encouraged us.
I wrote a play about
The Trojan War.
He pinned it on the wall,
For all to see.
I was so proud.
I liked Mr Birch.
He gave you confidence,
Encouraged creativity.
One of my best friends was
The worst artist in the class.
His people were stick men.
Mr Birch got him to draw
Some big ones,

Then turned them into
An amazing canvass,
Displayed on the wall.
A piece of modern art,
Embellishing the primitive.
My friend was,
Like me,
So proud.
Mr Birch was the definition
Of a brilliant teacher,
Bringing out the best
In everyone.
He painted the four houses on the wall,
In their gear.
Romans,
Normans,
Saxons,
Vikings.
So lifelike.
Romans were red,
Normans were green,
Saxons were blue,
Vikings were yellow.
I was a Roman prefect,
With my red prefect's badge.
Proud again.
What a good school
That made you so proud.
About yourself,
Your work,
Your House.
What a great teacher,
Mr Birch.

Pigs

We played our home games
On stony pitches,
By a village called Berengaria,
Just outside Limassol.
Berengaria was the wife
Of Richard the Lionheart,
The revered English king,
Who was French,
And was hardly ever in England,
As he was always on Crusades.
Which was where
He met Berengaria.
Next to our pitches
Was a hut.
A queue of pigs.
Bad things happened in that hut.
Pork was created.
The pigs knew it.
Not stupid, pigs.
I know that from
Watching them in Berengaria.
When its turn came,
Each pig resisted.
Two men pulled and pushed.
The pig howled.
And in the hut, screeched,
Wildly.
Then fell silent.
We played football
As all this happened.
And ate pork chops at home,
As you do.

Octopus/Shark

When I lived in Cyprus,
In Limassol,
My Dad worked at Akrotiri.
British sovereign territory
In an independent state.
He was in the angling club,
Which had its own beach.
And a raft,
To which we swam, and fished
For garfish and bream,
And rainbow fish,
And the occasional crazy
Tunny,
Which we call tuna now.
And we snorkelled,
With the raft as our base.
We'd dive for sea urchins,
Compete for the deepest dive,
Before we were even
Eleven.
At one with marine nature,
In a way that you just couldn't be,
In the colder climes
Of our home country.

One day an octopus grabbed my leg,
When I put my foot down a hole.
We caught it,
Iridescent as we hooked it
Out of the water,
With a stick.
Cruel.

But it grabbed my leg.
When I infringed its territory,
Admittedly.
I feel bad about it now,
But at the time,
It was an adventure.
And we sold it to the Greeks
For a Pound.

In September the sharks ventured
Closer to shore.
Or so we were told.
One evening,
As dusk drew in,
We saw a fin
By the raft.
No-one was out there still.
We were too afraid of the sharks,
Which no-one
Had ever seen.
But we saw one now.
The tell-tale fin,
Lurking,
Threatening.
We did the only thing
That boys could do.
We collected some rocks,
And hurled them at the fin,
Lurking in the dark haze.
It had no effect.
The shark remained.
We got bored,
And went back to the clubhouse,
Full of tall tales.
We'd attacked a shark,
It was definitely a shark.

We were buzzing.
And we hoped it wouldn't
Be there tomorrow.
Waiting to get
Its revenge.

Tornado

23 December 1969,
My party,
11th Birthday.
Born on Christmas Day.
Limassol,
Turkish restaurant,
Kebabs, mezze,
Loved it all.
Friends came to our house,
There's been a tornado.
Dad checked with the restaurant,
No answer.
The boys came round,
Tales of dustbins in front of houses
Stolen away.
Went down the high street,
Ripping rooves off.
No-one died,
Miraculously.
We saw a video at school,
The whirl of wind and water
Coming off the sea,
Dark and swirling.
All dark,
Foreboding,
Frightening,
Unthinkable.
What if you couldn't escape it?
What if it lifted you up,
And hurled you down
Into the road?
What if it filled you with air,

Like a balloon,
And then stuck a ten inch spike in
Your stomach,
And you went hurtling into space?
What if it took you out to sea,
And dropped you there to drown,
And be eaten by the sharks?
It didn't come down our street,
But my Mum had to make party food
Instead of us going to
The Turkish restaurant,
Which had been
Destroyed
By the tornado.
We had a good time,
Eating,
Singing,
Boasting,
Sniggering,
Our shadows in the shadows,
Flickering
In the candlelight.
But it wasn't the same.
Not often your party
Gets ruined
By a tornado.

Alan Hudson

I missed the first
Chelsea v Leeds Cup Final
At Wembley,
In 1970.
We were flying back to England,
From Cyprus,
After three years,
And the plane was delayed,
A lot.
I listened to the game on the radio,
The FA Cup mattered
A lot,
In those days.
And this one had
The Fancy London boys
Against the dirty Northern
Bastards.
It was 2-2,
On an incredibly muddy pitch.
Replay at Old Trafford,
Manchester.
Chelsea won 2-1.
A brutal game.
The 70s were like that.
A David Webb header won it.
The fancy dans beat the dirty bastards.
Much of the nation rejoiced.
No-one liked Leeds,
Unless they supported them.
And quite a lot of people did,
Even in Suffolk.

At school we played
Chelsea v Leeds
Every playtime,
In the playground,
With a tennis ball.
We were all a player.
I was Alan Hudson,
The silky skilled,
Long haired
Midfielder.
Full of promise,
A bit flaky.
I admired those silky skills,
And the flakiness,
Even at age 11.
Wanted to play like him,
Even though I knew,
By that age,
I was a natural defender.
Better at destroying
Than creating,
Apart from that occasional
Incisive pass.
Chelsea won more than Leeds
In the playground,
And Alan Hudson did his bit.
More than he ended up doing
For Chelsea,
Or England.
He was part of a group
Of gifted midfielders,
With long hair and
Bad attitudes,
That the managers
Never trusted.
Stanley Bowles,

Charlie George,
Tony Currie,
Frankie Worthington,
Rodney Marsh.
And Alan Hudson.
Between them, a handful of
England caps.
Lost talents,
Never trusted.
Typical England.
Our best talents discarded,
And two World Cups in the 70s
We failed
To qualify for,
While the great talents
Were wasted,
Ignored,
Never trusted.
And the hard workers,
The cloggers,
Were chosen instead.

But I was Alan Hudson
When we played
Chelsea v Leeds
And proud of it.

Football tears

The last,
And first,
Time
I ever cried
Over a football match
Was in 1970,
At the World Cup,
When we lost,
3-2,
To Germany.
After being
2-0 up,
In control,
The only team who could challenge
Brazil.
Destined for the Final,
For revenge,
After the unlucky
Group defeat.
Ramsey took Bobby Charlton off,
Beckenbauer was liberated.
We crumbled,
With Bonetti
(The Cat!)
In goal,
Because Banks was sick.
Even with Bonetti
It should never have happened.
It was like a bad dream.
How could it be so?
2-0 up.
Like torture.
2-1.

2-2.
2-3.
Out.
The end.
So abrupt,
So stupid.
I cried.
The start of the hurt
That has never gone away,
Watching England.
No more crying,
Though Gazza's tears in 1990
Almost did for me.
But so much disappointment,
And anger,
Fading to
Indifference.
Who cares?
The Premier League starts soon.
But in 1970,
We thought we could conquer
The world.
Again.

Kerry and the aeroplane

Something happened to me,
Between Cyprus and Suffolk.
Kerry lived further down my street.
Blonde,
Pretty,
Nice.
I liked her.
I made a model aeroplane,
Went out into the street,
To test it out.
Kerry came along,
Asked if she could have a go.
I said I had to go in.
Why?
She was so lovely,
I liked her.
I went in and watched
Saturday Grandstand,
Instead of getting to know Kerry
Better.
Why?

Leeds hooligan tsunami

When I was a young teenager,
My Dad took me to watch Ipswich
And Norwich.
We went to a Norwich-Leeds game once,
Leeds were a top side.
We hated them.
My Dad was Arsenal,
I was West Ham.
We agreed that Leeds
Were the dirtiest team in the League.
We were walking back to the station.
The chanting grew louder.
We froze.
A wave of people flowed,
Surged,
Past us.
Chanting obscenities,
Leeds songs.
We just stood still,
Assumed the crouch position,
Like we were in an air crash.
They passed through,
They disappeared into Woolworths,
To shoplift as they chose.
No police in sight.
We surveyed the scene.
An old man on the floor,
Stunned,
Walking stick askance,
Shocked.
People moved to help him,
We didn't have to.

But we would have done.

The damage of a day out
At the football.

Vera

The desks shuffle forward,
Vera has his back turned,
Scratching out something
About God
On the blackboard.
Surname's Lynn,
Hence the nickname.
White cliffs of Dover.
Shuffle, shuffle, sniggering.
I join in,
But
Feel deeply sorry
For the man,
The teacher,
Who is now trapped,
Imprisoned,
By his own pupils.
The frozen smile,
The fear.
I feel sorry for
Vera Lynn.
A good man,
A kind man,
In love with his subject.
With God.
But I'm as guilty
As the rest.
I joined in.

When I was little,
I wanted to be
A zookeeper.

That changed to
A teacher,
Until the day
We trapped Vera Lynn
With our desks.

I think he joined the clergy.

Gillian

Gillian sat behind me,
In class.
Third year,
When we'd gone comprehensive
In Bury St Edmunds.
Her Dad was the physics teacher.
He was so boring.
But Gillian was so beautiful.
Her dark eyes shone,
Glittered,
Hazel, chocolate, gold.
Her hair was brown.
She had poise,
A lovely smile.
I hardly ever
Spoke to her,
Even though she sat
Right behind me.
I was too scared
That she'd think I was
An idiot.
So I just smiled occasionally,
Said the odd word,
Which I can't now remember.
And just dreamed
Of telling her I was in love
With her,
And she telling me
She loved me
Too.
But it never happened.
I just imagined her beautiful eyes

Looking at the back
Of my head,
As we listened to her Dad
Droning on.

Open goal

Picked at centre forward.
Left or right back usually.
Solid,
Fast,
Not pretty.
Midfield aspirations.
But up front this time,
My chance for glory.
I run around a lot,
Going nowhere,
Blister on big toe,
Limping.
Team mate lofts the ball
Into my path.
Use my pace,
I'm on goal,
Just the keeper to beat,
My chance for glory.
Go round him
Or slot it in?
Oh the celebration,
As it goes in.
What if I miss?
The humiliation.
Just the keeper to beat.
My chance for glory,
Or shame.
Hero,
Villain,
Sniffer,
Chump.
Left or right?

Go round him,
Or slot it in?
Shit!
He's getting close.
Must shoot.
Go right,
Quick.
Snatched.
Ball curves,
Tamely,
Into the keeper's
Chest.
Rebounds.
Second chance.
Defender slides in,
We crash to the floor.
Penalty!
I look to the ref.
Impassive.
I silently implore him,
He silently ignores me.
Corner.
Just a poxy corner,
Instead of glory.
My chance for glory.
Over.
Back to left or right back
Next week.

Henry

Henry was our dog,
When I was a teenager.
A surly teenager,
Like most teenagers.
The ones I know, anyway.
Henry was surly too.
He didn't like strangers,
Or other dogs.
He went crazy in the car,
Barking at imaginary foe,
Out of the back window.
But his bark was so much worse
Than his bite.
He was the biggest coward
I knew,
After me,
Though I saw myself as
A writer,
Not a fighter,
After I saw an album cover
With that on it.
I stopped a few fights in my day.
Peace and love man.
Except on the football field,
Where I was a bit of a
Clogger.

Henry was half Alsatian,
Half terrier.
God knows how that happened.
He could run at
Greyhound speed,

After a ball,
Up to a football crossbar,
Or away from other dogs.
He didn't like other dogs.
No sniffing
In embarrassing places
For Henry.
I was his best friend.
I took him for walkies every night,
At 9.30pm,
After the News on the BBC.
I teased him with whispers.
He whinged and whined,
And was so happy
When I went to get his lead.

I once kicked a Jack Russell
Into the air,
When it tried to attack Henry,
On our morning walk.
All for one.
I'm sure he would have done the same
For me,
Even though
He was usually a coward.

Out of the blue,
My Dad got rid of him.
He started roaming,
That's true.
He gnawed the skirting boards,
But only when he was
On his own.
He was a weird dog
Really.
But he was my mate.

My Dad said that he took him
To a dogs' home,
But my sister and I didn't believe him.
We reckoned he was put down.
RIP Henry.
We still don't really know.

School on Saturday shock

We moved to Rutland,
Home of the Rutles,
And Ruddles County,
And Oakham School.
My Dad made sure
I got in there.
The Council paid.
Met the deputy housemaster.
Toad.
Do you play hockey he said?
Firsts at Bury I said.
That was football done for me.
Duped.
Saturday lessons were mentioned.
Saturday lessons?
Who has Saturday lessons?
Public schools, that's who.
What about Grandstand?
What about the FA Cup final build up?
What about sleep?
I did Saturday morning lessons for
The rest of my school life,
And sport in the afternoons.
Tea and sandwiches after
Valiant defeats,
And occasional thrashings,
All over
The East Midlands.
Hitched home
From school
Afterwards,
Singing songs from Diamond Dogs,

On the B668.
Rats as big as cats,
Mother in a whirl,
Boy or girl?
Bro-other,
Ooh, ooh,
Chigga, chigga!

Always got a lift too.

Different times.

The best rugby result ever

The best rugby result,
Ever,
Was Johnsons 0 Chapmans 0.
In the fifth form.
Day boys v borders,
Sweats v Poofs,
Lads v posh boys,
State v private,
Clever v stupid,
Or so we thought,
Being day boys.

They were better than us,
But we were hard.
A team.
No surrender.
It pissed with rain.
A quagmire.
Suited us.
Put in the tackles,
Held on to the ball,
Or hoofed it down the field,
And regrouped,
To repulse
The next assault.
The ref had no control.
There was low level violence,
Class conflict,
Sort of.
They hated us,
And we hated them.
Waves of attack,

Stopped
By fair means or foul.
The latter mostly.
Chapmans started arguing
Amongst themselves.
We knew then we were the winners,
Morally.
0-0.
The best rugby result ever.

First concert

My first concert ever
Was Status Quo,
At Leicester de Montfort Hall.
Right at the front,
I touched
Francis Rossi's plimsoll.
Down Down,
Roll Over Lay Down,
Caroline,
Paper Plane.
The thudding beat,
The riffs on repeat.
Thump, thump, thump.
Bang, bang, bang.
The circle visibly moving,
As everyone up there
Bounced in unison.
The essence of rock'n'roll.
I wrote to Sounds
On behalf of the lads.
Status Quo
Were fucking brilliant,
I said.
Signed Flob, Rollo, Pig, Morv, John.
They published it.

Fame!

Don't walk away

In a pub,
Leicester,
Melton Mowbray,
Somewhere,
With my mates,
My best mates.
Go to the loo,
My round soon.
Got no money.
Don't go back to the bar,
Go back to school.
On my own.
I walk away,
Just walk away.

I'm blank,
Some force I don't understand.
Could have just said,
Got no money,
I'll owe it,
No problem.
But I didn't,
I couldn't.
Even with my best mates,
I just walk away.

No-one says anything
The next day.
My best mates
Are still
My best mates
The next day.
Even though

I didn't stay.
Even though
I didn't say.
Even though
I just walked away.

I still don't know
Why I walked away
That day.
But at work, in life,
To this day,
If I'm feeling in an angry way,
Thinking fuck all this,
Why should I stay?
I always say,
Don't walk away.

That's not to say
I've never walked away
Since that day.
But think it through,
Stay cool, stay true,
Don't give it all away.
You usually find
You're feeling fine,
Back in line,
Soothed by time,
When you rise and shine,
At the start of another day.

Vambo O levels

I revised for
My O Levels
Listening to
The Sensational Alex Harvey Band.
The Impossible Dream mainly.
Not a good title
When you are taking exams.
Not good music
To relax to,
Or to soothe your soul.
But Vambo rooled,
For me, at sixteen.
Read the whole
Physics textbook.
I was crap at physics.
Read the textbook,
Cover to cover,
Wondering who was
The Man in the Jar.
Never found out,
But I got an A in physics.

Punk v Prog

The dayboy-border
Class War
Took many forms.
On the rugby field,
In A Level Economics,
And especially in music.
Punk v Prog.

For us:
Feelgoods,
Hot Rods,
Pistols,
Clash,
Stranglers,
Damned,
And still Bowie, always Bowie.

For them:
Peter fucking Frampton,
With that stupid vocoder,
Yes,
ELP,
Genesis,
Supertramp,
(How I loathed Crime of the Century)
Rick Wakeman.
Proper music,
They said.
People who could play their
Instruments,
Lots of instruments.
Big deal.

They were still shit.

Flob stuck with Sabbath,
Oblivious to all trends.
Good on him.
He's probably still rocking
To Masters of Reality
To this very day.

We agreed with the boarders
On a few things.
The majesty of Led Zep,
The many wonders of Kate Bush,
The joys of Bob Marley,
Soul music when you wanted to dance,
With girls.
And I had a guilty pleasure,
Crossed sides.
I liked Genesis.
Not even the cool
Peter Gabriel Genesis
(That was too prog for me
Apart from the lawn mower song)
But the Phil Collins Genesis,
When he first took over
The vocals.
Twist of the Tail,
Wind and Wuthering.
NME adverts for these
Adorned my walls,
Alongside the punk,
And the pub rock,
And Kate Bush,
Beautiful
In her blue leotard.

No-one cared that I liked Genesis,
The class war wasn't real.
We were all privileged
Going to that school,
And we knew it.
But you have to posture when
You are seventeen.
And I still like those
Genesis albums,
Though I hate their eighties stuff.
That's another story.

English

I loved English.
At school it was
My favourite A level,
Even if I chose economics
For university,
In the end.
I loved the creativity,
The insight into human kind.
The mysteries of
T.S.Eliot's masterpiece,
The Wasteland.
April is the cruellest month,
Stetson! You who were with me
In the ships at Mylae!
The opulence,
And the breakdowns,
In Tender is the Night.
Nicole and Dick,
Fortunes reversed.
The magnificent tragedies
Of Othello,
And Lear.
The green eyed monster,
The self-inflicted misfortune,
The rage,
Defeat,
Inevitable and final.
Walking back from supper,
With class mates,
Exclaiming,
Howl wind, crack your cheeks!
Actions speak louder than words,

But words last longer than actions.

I didn't spend all my time,
As a teenager,
Pining after girls
I was too shy to ask out,
Because I was in love with words.
The Clash,
T.S Eliot,
Shakespeare,
Orwell,
Tolstoy,
F.Scott Fitzgerald,
Conrad,
Apocalypse Now,
(You surf or you fight!)
David Byrne,
Alex Harvey,
Elvis Costello,
Bruce Springsteen.
Slogans,
Observations,
Metaphors,
Emotions,
Resonances,
Fragments,
Memories.

Words.

English.

If you leave me now

If you leave me now,
By Chicago,
Was a smoochy ballad
I'd normally despise.
But it was *the*
Smoochy ballad
Of the time.
Up there with
I'm not in Love,
By 10 cc.
And it was
The smoochy ballad
That I danced to
With Amanda,
At her party,
In the holidays.
My chance
To tell her
How much I liked her.
(I was scared of mentioning love.)
And I told her,
As we held each other,
Amid the slow grooves
Of Chicago's finest moment.
She smiled her
Lovely dimpled smile,
And said thank you,
With a look of sympathy.
And I smiled back,
Like it was
No big deal.
Torn up inside.

We finished the dance,
We hugged.
We stayed friends.

Get out of Denver baby

Roll out of the bunk bed,
Have a shower.
Tasteless breakfast.
Chapel, maybe Jerusalem.
Back to room.
Get out of Denver baby,
Go go go!
Get out of Denver,
Eddie and the Hot Rods,
Live at the Marquee,
Singing Bob Seger's song
At 100 miles an hour.
Exam.
Nondescript lunch.
Back to room.
Get out of Denver baby,
Go go go!
96 Tears.
Exam.
Over for the day.
Back to room.
Get out...
No maybe a bit of Kate Bush.
Supper,
Pub,
Revision.
Repeat next day.
Rock'n'roll
Inspired me through A Levels,
And inspires me
In the same way,
To this day.

Without football

First morning.
Staring at the ceiling.
What do I do now?
No friends,
No family.
In a room.
People next door.
Say hello.
My new friends?
Who knows?
Stay in after
Supper,
Read Dostoevsky.
(True)
What now?
Monday comes.
Football training.
Meet some people,
My kind of people,
Down the pub,
Friends for life.
What would I do
Without football?

Posh dinner

When I went up to Oxford,
Up not down, that's the clue,
I had no idea
What to do.
I met a Scotsman
Called Donald.
He was a good mate.
He invited me to
A Burns night dinner.
It was black tie.
I borrowed one from someone.
I didn't have the money
To hire one,
Though I had discovered
The overdraft
By then.
At dinner I sat opposite
This posh guy who
Had been President
Of the JCR.
Cool.
There were five implements on each side
Of the plate.
Work in from the outside,
I knew that.
But would it be enough?
I watched the posh guy
Carefully.
He knew what to do,
I was OK.

SDLP vs SWP

I tried politics
At Oxford.
Went to the Union.
Twats.
(Though the discos were good.)
Joined the Social Democratic Labour
Party.
(Ahead of its time.)
Met a couple of decent people.
Went to a meeting
With the Socialist Workers,
To debate how to deal
With the National Front.
We said democracy,
They said violence.
What a surprise!
Bought a paper from an SWP type.
Socialist solidarity.
He took my money and said,
Sucker.
What a wanker.
Asked myself,
Why am I here?
Could be in the pub,
With the lads.
And that's what I did
For the rest of my time
At Oxford.
Football,
Pub,
Discos,
Study, lots of study,

Friends.
Not spending time
With a bunch of tossers,
Thinking they were following
In the footsteps
Of Trotsky,
Or Churchill,
Or anyone else
For that matter.
Strange breed,
Politicians.

Coat

Just before I went to Oxford,
I went with my Dad to Norwich,
And he bought me some clothes.
I already had a suit.
Brown pinstripe,
Hideous,
With massive lapels,
And flares.
But at the time
It was cool.
I got some jeans,
Tried straights,
As punk was in.
Thought I looked
Like a stick insect,
And bought flares again.
Massive error!
I got a coat too,
Black Crombie style.
Double breasted.
Felt good.
I wore it with my
West Ham scarf,
And Doc Martens,
Cherry Red.
And for a while those flares,
(The last flares I ever wore).

I was in the College main quad
One day.
A posh chap,
Someone I knew

Quite well,
Came up to me
And said,
"Sills I like that coat,
Can I buy it off you?"
Off my back?
Who did he think I was?
Some poor chump,
Who'd sell his clothes
To a rich boy?
I can't remember exactly what I said,
But it was no.
Should have been
Fuck off.
But I wouldn't have wanted
To cause a scene.

When I think about it now,
It's even worse.
The audacity,
The arrogance.
The rich kid thinking,
I'll do this simple lad
A favour,
By buying the coat
Off his back.

Fuck off!

Bruce

Home for the holidays.
In bed listening to Radio 3.
The late show, showcasing
Modern artists
For the classical listeners.
On comes this song,
Racing in the Street.
My mind blown.
Lying in the dark.
Met her on the strip three years ago,
Now she's on her Daddy's porch,
Looking like she wished
She'd never been born.
While those guys,
Who don't give up living,
Go racing in the streets.
Simple, melancholy keys,
Echo of the sixties' joyful past,
Turned dark.
I'm mesmerised.
In the dark,
Under the covers.
My life has changed.
I knew Bruce before,
Celebrated Bruce before,
But now I believe.
An Oxford boy,
Stuck in Norfolk,
Grasping at that something
That he don't understand.
An awakening,
In the dark,

Girls barefoot in the park.
Drinking warm beer
In the soft summer rain.
Metaphors
That speak
To all time and place.
All feelings.
Bruce formed a backdrop,
From that moment.
Helped me to understand,
Explain,
My anger,
My frustration,
And my love.
The soundtrack
To my life
Can be measured out,
Not in in coffee spoons,
But in Springsteen songs.
Bruce is a true American.
The Boss.
Spokesman for the
Working man,
But spokesman too,
For something
That is universal.
Love, respect, integrity.
Adversity,
Aspiration,
Fulfilment.
The Promised Land?

Escargots s'il vous plait

I'm eating snails in Antibes,
In the Marche Provençale.
2015.
Reminds me of the first time,
Eating snails,
In Paris.
1978.
With Donald,
Courtesy of a man from Martini.
We went to a restaurant,
On the Champs d'Elysees,
Dead posh it was.
Like nothing I'd ever
Been to before.
I ordered snails and steak,
Because that seemed
The right thing to do.
In France.
We got these contraptions
To eat the snails.
I wasn't sure what to do with them,
But it looked like you gripped
The shell
With one thing,
And poked out the snail
With the other.
When they arrived I tried it.
It was quite tricky at first.
But then it got easy.
I was a proper gourmand.
Escargots s'il vous plait,
Set up for life.

Don't forget to dip your bread
Into the garlic butter.
Otherwise
Snails don't taste of much.

Police and Thieves

At Oxford, I bought my records
In two places.
A second hand shop
On the High Street,
Where I offloaded old favourites,
To pay for the new.
And a place in
Little Clarendon Street.
Obscure but vital.
Loved to browse there,
Always something good
On the stereo.
Finally got my copy
Of The Clash's first album
There in '78.
And then the greatest
Twelve inch
Of all time,
Junior Murvin's
Police and Thieves.
Four versions.
The vocal
So sweet,
As Junior sang
Of violence and mayhem,
Scaring the nation,
With their guns and ammunition.
Against that wonderful,
Lilting,
Reggae beat.
The toasting,
The saxophone,

The dubwise exploration.
Versions.
A revelation.
Took me on a journey beyond
Bob Marley,
Always and forever
The inspiration.
The Live album,
Then Exodus,
Set me on the path
To revelation,
Reggae revolution.
The Clash took me further,
Pointed me to Junior Murvin.
Police and Thieves,
On that first Clash album.
Covered with respect,
And style.
The Clash played reggae
Like it was ingrained
In their souls,
And encouraged
White boys like me
To immerse themselves
In the sounds of
Jamaica.
Another love affair
That has never ended.
And that Junior
Twelve inch
Still takes
Centre stage.
The sweetest lament,
The coolest rhythm.

Level vibes seen?

The lone tree

Summers in Norfolk.
Flat.
The land,
The life.
Went cycling a lot,
Dreamed of Oxford,
And unattainable girls.
Listened to Bruce,
And the Clash,
Read economics,
And Tolstoy.
Anna Karenina, War and Peace.
Immersed.
Went out on my bike,
With my Olympus Trip.
Captured the unassuming
Beauty
Of the landscape.
The detail.
A single tree
Looked on,
Gnarled,
Alone,
Ancient,
Magnificent.
No need for company.
Lord of the manor.
The hedgerows and ditches,
Amber fields,
Rich soils,
The swish of crops,
Bending with the breeze.

A warble in the branches,
A rustle in the undergrowth,
The click of the camera,
Otherwise no sound.
Serene.
Barely a car,
Or tractor,
In sight.
Just the lone tree
Unchallenged,
Rooted,
Unyielding,
Confident
In its own company.

A lesson.
An example.
An inspiration.

Playing to win

Frosty February.
Ground rock hard.
They didn't postpone games
In those days.
Two-all,
Holding on
To that unbeaten
Record.
Ed on the touch line,
Shivering.
75 minutes,
Holding on,
Fighting hard.
Ed trembling.
We score.
Three-two.
Top of the league,
Batten down the hatches.
Ed clattering.
Game over,
Victory!
Top of the league.
Where's Ed?
Oh well,
Winning is what
It's all about.
He turned up for the
Next game,
Played well.
Not sure I ever
Apologised
For leaving him

Shivering, trembling, clattering,
For 90 minutes,
On a frosty February.

Bit late now.

Blue dress

I spent a weekend
With you,
In your house in Cambridge once.
We played croquet,
And your mother
Made us a really nice dinner.
I can't remember anything else,
Except that I wanted to tell you
I loved you.
But I knew it would be futile,
Because you were
Going out
With one of my friends,
And I never imagined
I could (or should) usurp him.
But we used to dance together.
At college,
And afterwards,
For quite a while,
Until we lost touch.
Most of the lads
Didn't like dancing,
But I did,
Especially when it was
With you.

Much later,
We danced again.
You had a blue dress on,
And the sweat showed,
As it always does with blue.
Because you'd already

Been doing your thing,
On the dancefloor.
We danced again.
And I remembered the
Times past,
And was happy,
Because things worked out
For me, as well as you.
So the memory
Was fond,
Not sad.
Teenage love.
But I still wanted to hug you
At the end.
A hug for the past, as well as
The present.
And I did hug you,
Feeling your damp blue dress,
And the beating heart
Beneath it.

Gordon's lesson

Gordon was my first boss,
Big Boss.
Perry was in between.
Gordon and Perry recruited me,
And the other boys.
Gordon loved his boys.
Corporate planning,
Economics,
BP,
1980.
Thatcher,
Economic turmoil,
Oil price explosion,
OPEC.
Made it interesting.
I wrote a country analysis
About the Middle East.
Gordon called me in.
My effort was
Turgid, and boring.

Turgid and boring?

The worst insult.
Crap, wrong, all OK.
Not turgid, and boring.
I sulked,
I was dismissed.
I was called back.
John you have to
Let it breathe,
Let it breathe, yes!

No student essays,
No clever phrases.
Play it straight,
Simple,
Short sentences
And paragraphs.
Crisp language.
Readers with little time.
Think of the reader,
Strip to the essence,
Maximise impact.
I learned.
Never forgot
The day
Gordon said
My work was
Turgid,
And boring.

Minibus crusade

Had money,
But no friends,
To holiday with.
Took a minibus,
With a bunch of people
I didn't know.
From Dover
To Istanbul,
Via Munich,
Graz,
Belgrade,
The Greek border,
Thassos.
Camping,
Drinking,
Singing,
Drinking,
Sightseeing,
Drinking.
A route
The Crusaders
Might have taken,
Bringing death and destruction,
Rape and pillage,
In their wake.
We just drank beer and sang songs.

I fell in love
With Lindsey,
From Rochdale.
Dark wavy hair,
And hazel eyes,

And a lovely smile.
Danced with her
In Istanbul,
Living the dream.
Sang Beatles songs
On the Greek border,
To represent England.
Steered clear of the Birdy Song
In Graz.
Enjoyed Munich Beerfest
So much,
That I have no real memory of it.
Except from the photos.

But I know Lindsey was
Always there,
Always close by,
Always in my dreams.

Saw her in London
A couple of times,
With the gang.
We stayed in touch.
I offered to come up North,
For the weekend.

She was busy.

The girl with the
Spanish eyes

I took you to a dinner dance.
BP did that sort of thing
In 1982.
I knocked on your door.
You answered,
So beautiful,
Dark hair, red ribbons,
Red dress that hugged your shape,
Which was perfect.
And those Spanish eyes.
Did I think of them
In those terms
At the time?
Maybe not.
Bono sang about a girl with
Spanish eyes
Much later.
I completely understood
What he meant.
And you were so
Beautiful
That night.
We drank, ate, danced.
I twirled you round to some
Rock'n'roll,
And thought
I was in heaven.
I also felt sick,
Leaping around,
Too much to drink,
And in love.

I had to stop,
For a moment.
Not good, but
Didn't seem to do any harm.
I got invited back for coffee.
We talked,
But not about what
I really wanted
To talk about.
I just couldn't say
What I wanted to say.
And after a while you said,
It's time for you to go.
And I did.
Gutted.
I went home and played
Darkness on the Edge of Town,
With a Jack Daniels and ice.
And hoped we could
Go out again.

Hat

Fiona joined us,
For reasons I forget.
Work experience probably.
She was eighteen
And beautiful.
Wavy blonde hair
In a twenties style cut.
Pale blue eyes
(Linger on).
It was her birthday.
Steve and I decided
We must buy her
A hat.
We headed for Oxford Street
In our lunch break,
To start off with anyway.
It took us ages
To find
The right hat.
We tried them all on
In the Ladies' sections
Of the department stores.
How does this one look?
Not you darling.
What about Fiona?
Maybe.
How about this one?
A few odd looks,
But it's London,
Anything goes.

We found
The one.
White and wide brimmed.
Fiona looked
Sensational in it.
She lived in deepest Sussex.
I took her out one Saturday,
To an Indonesian in Soho,
And walked her back
To Charing Cross,
Arm in arm.
Kissed her as she got onto the train.
Knew that was all.
Wallowed in the bliss,
The unachievable.
But alright, because I knew
It would be like that.
Sweet pain,
As the train pulled away.
My movie scene.
No steam,
But a cloud of regret.
And then she left BP,
And that was that.
And so did Steve,
For much
Greater things.

The Aardvarks

We played five-a-side,
Monday lunch times.
Squeezing in the BP lunch
Afterwards.
Two courses for 5p,
With a slab of ice cream
On your custard,
If you wanted it.
Feeling a bit sleepy
After all that.
But we never had too much to do
In those
Halcyon days.

We entered a team into
The BP five-a-side,
Down at Sydenham,
Deep South,
On a Tuesday evening.
We called ourselves
The Aardvarks,
In the hope we'd get some early games,
And get to the pub,
After the inevitable defeats,
Inflicted
By the refinery boys,
And the explorers.
We were just a bunch of
Economists
From head office.
With skimpy shorts,
Eighties-style,

And t-shirts with
A green and yellow aardvark
On the front,
Which probably looked
Like we were taking the piss.
We were hammered,
As expected.
There were clashes,
Heavy tackles,
No quarter given.
But we consoled ourselves
That we probably
Earned the most.

Being the Aardvarks didn't work.
We might as well have been the Zebras.
And there was only time
For a snatched pint,
Before escaping back to
London.

Where we ruled.

Bristol

Bristol.
A great city.
Great music.
Home of Massive Attack,
Home of the Big Man,
Early eighties.
Minor mayhem.
World wine fairs, beer fests,
Greek restaurants.
3 am,
Smashing plates on heads.
Dancing round the handbags
At some nightclub.
Big Man taking off his shoes
When the girls did.
End of dance!
Scrumpy bars,
Gareth ejected,
Banned.
Street songs.
In Every Dream Home a Heartache.
Inflatable doll,
Ringing through the suburbs.
Big Man staying on at a party,
Locked out of his own flat,
Me and Smithy,
Blissfully asleep,
While he pissed
In a phone box,
To keep warm.
Bristol.
Such fine memories!

Walthamstow

End of the Victoria Line.
Spurs is Seven Sisters.
Not much call to go further.
Been to Walthamstow twice.
Early eighties,
The dogs after work.
Glitzy stadium,
US-style.
The Big Man said,
Watch out for dogs crapping,
Been fed to lose.
We watched out for dogs crapping,
And lost all our bets.
Second time,
First leg of a stag do,
Friends of the Big Man.
Fight breaks out,
Fairly minor,
Over quickly.
Big Man and I go off to the loo.
Friends gone when we return.
Walk back to Finsbury Park,
As you do.
Next morning,
Victoria station,
Bound for Brighton.
Big Man's friends arrive.
Battered,
Bruised,
Cuts on faces,
Black eyes.
Followed out of pub,

Attacked,
While Big Man and I
Strolled
Merrily
Back to Finsbury Park.
Lucky.
Never rushed to get back
To Walthamstow.

Thank you

The first time I asked you out
Was one of those rare moments
When I got decisive,
With a girl I liked.
We were talking about the dinner dance.
Your friend,
Fellow secretary,
Was there too.
And one of my mates
From the office.
Your friend was going with her
Boyfriend.
You and I had no plans.
You thought I preferred her to you.
She disappeared for a moment,
My mate went for drinks.
My moment.
I asked you if you'd go with me.
You looked down,
With those beautiful shy eyes,
Then up.
And said yes.
We stayed on when our friends left.
I put my arm around you,
And promised you'd always
Been the one.

It lasted four months.
A lifetime for me,
But also cruelly short.
It was so good at first,
The best I'd ever felt.

It seemed that way for you too.
But somehow things went wrong.
My friends.
My attitude.
My insensitivity.
These were all undoubtedly
Factors.
I was so delighted
At having a proper relationship,
That I forgot that
It was for two people.
I fucked up,
And you couldn't cope.
So you did what was best for you,
And called it off.

I found it hard to understand that
What I treasured so much
Slipped so quickly from
My grasp.
I analysed a multitude of reasons,
I blamed all sorts of things,
And people.
And then Stevie Wonder
Gave me the answer.
I'll blame it on the sun,
The stars and the moon at night...
But heart blames it on me.
Yes me.
It was only me.
24.
Not ready to understand
The needs
Of another person.
A companion.
A lover, but also

A friend.

But thank you.
Because you were the first person
I ever loved in the way that
Lovers do.
And you showed
That someone could care for me
As much as I cared for them.
That requited love was a possibility,
A reality.

And although it broke my heart
To lose you,
It also,
In time,
Strengthened me.
Gave me confidence
That I could find love.
And I did.
And I think you did too.
So the pain
Was worth it.
At least for me.
Because I learned
A few lessons
About sensitivity,
And understanding.
And about sharing
Experiences.
Too late for us,
But good for the future.

Life's lessons.

Growin' up.

Lost in music / 1983

Went out with a girl,
Discovered a new world.
Lost the girl,
Lost that world.
But what was the old world?
Where was the old world?
Who was the old world?
Lost in London,
Lost in a whirl.

Lost in music.
Could be myself there.
Work out the truth there.
Be someone else there.

Bruce sang for me.
U2 inspired me.
Stevie answered me.
Style Council soothed me,
As the Long Hot Summer
Passed me by.
Hip hop intrigued me.
Camden Palace,
Searching for the perfect beat.
Dance entranced me,
And grooved me,
Searching for the perfect beat.
Lyceum, Friday night,
Grey loafers,
White socks,
Beer in hand,
Watching those beautiful

Suburban girls
Glide.

Pimlico rescued me
From self-pity.
No time for self-pity
When there's a party,
Or the Orange Brewery.
Music wars,
Of the friendly kind.
Grandmaster Melle Mel or Elvis C?
U2's Pride or Let it Be?
Hey!
They all belong to me!

New Year's Eve,
Dancing tight
With everyone
But the girl
Who liked me,
Who'd listened to me,
Talk endlessly
About my 1983.
Sorry,
Still sorry.
Not the real me.
Couldn't be the real me.

Except it was
Me.

You!
Yes you, yes me sir.
Hypocrite lecteur!
Mon sembable,
Mon frere!

And I don't know why,
Except a new dawn was nigh.
1984,
Gazing up at
The starry depths
Of a country sky.
I felt free,
Felt a new liberty.

From the

Peaks
     and
          troughs
of

1983.

(With acknowledgement to T.S.Eliot –
The Wasteland of course)

Balham

Party time.
Balham.
South London,
Sarf London.
Not my patch.
Feels alien,
Dark, foreboding.
Those Northern Line
Platforms
With no walls.
Used to go down to Morden
In 1983.
Grim.
Took ages.
But it was for my girl.
My ex-girl.

Across the room,
A girl with those
Spanish eyes
Again.
Graceful dancing.
I talk and talk
To my mates.
Like to.
Should.
Maybe.
Later.
All talk,
No action.
Have another beer.
And watch,

Always watching.

My friend goes over.
Bastard!
Can't let him do that.
Galvanized.
Not thinking now,
Not overthinking now.
Doing.
Acting.
Reacting.
Say hello.
Muscle friend out.
Out!
And we talk,
And talk,
And talk.
Talking's OK now.
Talking's so easy,
How did it become
So easy?

Life's random moments
That lead to
The big moment.
What you've been dreaming of.
Even though
You don't know it
At the time.

Carpe diem.
The rest takes care
Of itself.

When I met your friends

When I met your friends,
For the first time
After we met,
It was in Guildford.
There was a party
Where they lived.
I remember enjoying it
And liking them.
But most of all I remember the carpet.
It was really sticky.

Australians in Europe

The Fall had a song called
Australians in Europe.
B-side to Hit the North,
On my 12 inch single.
It had two lines.
One was Australians in Europe.
I can't remember the other.
But it wasn't complimentary.
Not that Mark E. Smith
Compliments
Anyone or anything.
But two of my best friends,
From the last forty years,
Are Australians in Europe.
They were in '84
And they are now.
Angela and Ginette.
Pimlico flat mates.
Married Irish architects.
Frank and Shane.
One love to you all.
The best.

23778902R00057

Printed in Great Britain
by Amazon